Three

Days

with

Joyce

Three

Days

with

Joyce

Photographs

by

Gisèle

Freund

gisèle freund (signature)

Preface

by

Richard

Ellmann

Persea

Books

New

York

Photographs and text by Gisèle Freund
originally published as *Trois Jours Avec Joyce*
(Editions Denoël, Paris, 1982).

© 1985 by Gisèle Freund
Translation © 1985 by Persea Books, Inc.
Preface © 1985 by Richard Ellmann
All rights reserved.
For information, address the publisher:
Persea Books
225 Lafayette Street
New York, N.Y. 10012

Translated by Peter St. John Ginna
Designed by Arnold Skolnick

Set in Gill Sans by Adroit Graphic Composition, New York
Printed by the Studley Press, Dalton, Massachusetts
Bound by the Book Press, Brattleboro, Vermont

Preface

Gisèle Freund found a great subject, and James Joyce a great photographer. Joyce had a keen sense of how he wished to present himself to posterity. Fiction was his business and he kept to it. Not for him to become known as a man of letters —the phrase repelled him. He wrote no prefaces nor, except in early youth, reviews of other people's books. He also declined interviews and, for the most part, photographs. However intimately his books engaged his readers, his private manner with the public was elaborately formal. He was willing to give help, but insisted it be unacknowledged, to Stuart Gilbert for a book on *Ulysses,* and to other friends for a book on *Work in Progress* (later disclosed to be *Finnegans Wake*). This help took the form of hints rather than prescriptions. When Herbert Gorman offered to write a biography, Joyce agreed, then provided such scant information that Gorman, within that scantness, had little freedom to wave his arms.

At the two times that Gisèle Freund photographed him, which were the spring of 1938 and the spring of 1939, Joyce was more receptive than usual to having his image recorded for posterity. The publication of *Finnegans Wake* —which he considered to be his greatest work—was at last imminent. He had begun it in 1922, soon after *Ulysses* had appeared. The composition dragged on for seventeen years, as against ten for *A Portrait of the Artist as a Young Man* and seven for *Ulysses.* There had been a forlorn hope of publishing it on his fifty-sixth birthday, 2 February 1938. Nothing happened and another year passed. Joyce saw an advance copy on his fifty-seventh birthday, but official publication did not take place until 4 May 1939.

Several causes protracted the period of the book's

composition. One was that the problems Joyce set himself in it were vast and intricate. This time he had no Homeric epic, as in *Ulysses,* against which to counterpose his own structure. Then there were his external circumstances. His health was unsteady. The years during which he wrote *Finnegans Wake* were also the years during which he submitted to ten operations for glaucoma and related complications. Though never blind, he was never unhampered in his sight.

Another cause of delay was the illness of his daughter. Lucia, born in 1907, began in adolescence to show signs of schizophrenia. At first Joyce assumed these were simply girlish ways, but about 1930 the signs multiplied. For the next decade much of his time and concern were lavished upon her plight. For a long time he denied that she was insane; he preferred to regard her as a Cassandra, and gave instances of her prophetic powers. Then as her condition deteriorated he tried various cures, such as injections of sea water, glandular treatments, visits to friends in far-off places, psychotherapy by C.G. Jung and other doctors, internments in various *maisons de santé.* Lucia only got worse. In the late 1930s Joyce finally acknowledged that she must be kept under treatment away from home. In her absence he continued to brood on her sufferings.

The third cause of delay was the criticism which *Finnegans Wake* began to receive even before its publication as a book, when fragments from it appeared in reviews. This criticism came from friends and critics alike. Of course Joyce had devotees who believed he could do no wrong, or anticipated that all the mysteries would be made plain once the whole work was available, or welcomed his opaqueness as a badge of modernism. But most people took a different view.

Few writers have been so confident as Joyce, but even he flinched at what was being said. He took particular offense at objections from writers with whom he had been friends, such as Wyndham Lewis and above all, Ezra Pound. They found no value in what he was doing. Even T. S. Eliot, though he had contracted for his firm, Faber & Faber, to publish the completed book, allowed a hostile review of one section of it to appear in the *Criterion,* of which he was editor, so Joyce could not feel sure of his allegiance, either.

Joyce found himself also to be on rather bad terms with the three women who had most advanced his career. Harriet Weaver, the publisher of *A Portrait of the Artist* and his longtime patron, felt compelled to tell him that he was wasting his genius. Sylvia Beach, who had published *Ulysses,* and Adrienne Monnier, who had published its French translation, conveyed to him that his zeal to publicize and profit from *Finnegans Wake* was out of proportion to the book's potential sale. Joyce's other friends mostly defended him, but some conceded privately that the book was fearfully obscure.

For his part, Joyce made little effort to defend himself. He would leave praise and castigation to others. He did allow, however, in writing to Miss Weaver, that "One great part of every human existence is passed in a state which cannot be rendered sensible by the use of wideawake language, cutanddry grammar, and goahead plot." The night world, with its fantasies, dreams, shadows, had a right to be unclear. He also emphasized that the book was funny ("*in risu veritas*") and that it was musical. But while he was defiant, and tenacious, he was also depressed, and worked more slowly. At last, however, he wrote the final pages, in which the freshwater river dies into the salt sea to inaugurate a new cycle, and he felt some triumph at having overcome all his difficulties.

This background may help to illuminate the situation in which Joyce was at the time that Gisèle Freund undertook to photograph him. Other elements of his extraordinary personality may also be glimpsed in her admirable images. It is sometimes assumed that Joyce was like his own Stephen Dedalus, addicted to stinging epigrams and acerbic rebuffs. In fact he was more convivial than Stephen and took pleasure in conversing, like his Leopold Bloom, on any number of subjects, whether with the hall porter or with someone famous. With his friends he liked to dine, though he ate little, and to drink, alcohol being his means to forsake temporarily his elegant formality. In his slow, meditative manner he would confide his troubles, and was pleased and sympathetic when friends confided theirs. With women he was unexpectedly prudish; alone with men he sometimes composed limericks. At parties, which he loved, he would smile and joke and do high kicks with great dexterity. He also liked to sing in his sweet though weak tenor, and would entertain with Irish songs or operatic arias. An inch or two short of six feet, he tended when he walked to curl up—as he said—like a question mark. He thought of himself as fragile, though in fact he was tough. His iron affections were confined to his family, that is, to his wife, Nora; his daughter Lucia; his son George; and George's wife, Helen, and their son Stephen. Gisèle Freund's photographs of Joyce and his grandson are among her most brilliant and moving. Of his friends Joyce required great loyalty, but did not repose much confidence in them.

Gisèle Freund had come at a lucky moment. As the

prospects of a second world war materialized, there was no more time for photographs. Joyce was alarmed, especially for Lucia. He had never established a permanent home in Paris, not even in nineteen years, and was uncertain where to go or to transfer his daughter if departure from France proved necessary. The war distressed him also because he feared, correctly, that it would distract the world from reading his book. For almost all his adult life he had kept aloof from politics, and by this time was averse to all governments. Hitler and Mussolini with their nationalistic frenzies and persecutions were especially repugnant to him. He was happy to help some of his former pupils and their relatives or friends to escape from the Nazis and resettle elsewhere. In late December of 1939 the Joyces went to Unoccupied France, near Vichy. In December of the following year he and his family managed to get to Zurich, where he died a month later. Gisèle Freund's photographs, formal and informal, are now part of his history.

—Richard Ellmann

Three

Days

with

Joyce

My first meeting with James Joyce was in 1936. Adrienne Monnier had invited me to a dinner party that she was giving in honor of the American playwright Thornton Wilder, who was passing through Paris. He was eager to make the acquaintance of the author of Ulysses, *a book he greatly admired; so Adrienne Monnier had invited "Mister Joyce." The other guests were Sylvia Beach and Maurice Saillet. Adrienne's charming, low-ceilinged apartment at 18 rue de l'Odeon was almost across the street from her bookstore, La Maison des Amis des Livres. Adrienne enjoyed at that time an extraordinary reputation and influence. All the best writers of the period—one particulary rich in literary talent—frequented her little shop, and Adrienne was a close friend of most of them: Paul Valèry, André Gide, Valery Larbaud, Léon-Paul Fargue, T. S. Eliot, Hemingway, and so many others. It was not only because she sold their books, but because they appreciated her profound understanding of the craft of literature, her astute and pungent observations. She herself was quite a gifted writer. "Nothing is more difficult," she remarked to me, "than to write the way you speak"; but André Gide once wrote to her, "One doesn't 'read' you so much as hear you talk, for you have managed to give your sentences the most natural tone of voice." Someone should republish her books, which give a unique picture of the literary life between the wars.*

To her bookshop, she had added a lending library and a small publishing house. Many students, myself among them, were members of the library. Guided by her knowledge, we read the avant-garde literature that had seemed reserved for an élite. I was about twenty years old then and I was studying sociology and the history of art. To pay for my studies, I had begun to do photographic journalism and portraits, using a little Leica my father had given me some years before. I had no idea, at the time, that photography would become my profession.

Joyce arrived accompanied by his wife, Nora, who was very beautiful. He was quite tall and thin, and already a bit stooped. And yet he was only fifty-three years old. He felt his way as he walked, no doubt because he could see very poorly. I knew he had undergone several operations for his vision. He was elegantly dressed in a light-colored suit and wore a bow tie. His forehead was high and his brown hair was sleek, though already graying and thinning. His mouth, with its very thin lips, looked like a cleft in his bony face.

The dinner passed in a gay and relaxed atmosphere, thanks to the Swiss white wine from Valais, Joyce's favorite. As I watched the author, I began to think of photographing him. I even dared to speak to him about it, but Joyce pleaded his work, his health, his poor eyesight. I didn't insist.

Two years later, in 1938, Finnegans Wake was due to be published and Life magazine asked me for photos of Joyce. His reputation, of course, had crossed the Atlantic; but there were no good portraits of him, except for the portraits that Man Ray and Berenice Abbot had taken years earlier. To persuade Joyce to sit for me, I addressed myself to his friend, the writer and distinguished journalist Louis Gillet. I asked him to explain to Joyce that a photo-essay about him could do much to aid the distribution of his latest work, which was written in language even more difficult than that of Ulysses.

Finally Joyce accepted. Indeed, he had very precise ideas about what sort of pictures I should take of him. And so, over several sessions, I succeeded in capturing a few moments of his life.

The publication of Finnegans Wake was eventually postponed for a year, and Time in New York asked me to do a portrait of Joyce in color for the cover of the magazine. I have written in The World and My Camera of those two memorable sittings.

Joyce was satisfied with my work. I showed him all the photographs, except those of him stepping out of the taxi. Knowing that he would arrive in rue de l'Odéon at about three in the afternoon, I had positioned myself in the street, near the entrance to Adrienne's bookshop. Joyce did not notice that I was photographing him, but he sensed that someone was hovering nearby. However, he did not recognize me. These photos were taken in the classic style of the paparazzi— twenty years before they came on the scene.

Nor did I show Joyce the color portrait in which he is seen head-on. I found it too revealing and tragic and I did not wish to upset him. It appears here for the first time in color.

First

Day

Joyce

at

Work

Eugene Jolas, born in the United States, writer, translator and critic, came to Paris in the twenties, accompanied by his lovely wife, Maria. They soon became the best friends of Joyce and his family.

Publishers of the avant-garde review
Transition, *the Jolases startled the*
literary world when, in the very first
issue of the magazine, in 1927, they
published sections of a book by Joyce:
Work in Progress, *later titled*
Finnegans Wake.

They believed in his genius. Eugene
Jolas often helped Joyce correct his
proofs, and Maria, as she has told with
considerable humor, acted as "the good
housekeeper," supervising the printing.

(handwritten annotations at top) Mona Vera Toutou Ipostaffair my Lsyg & Lysg mortinatality or

for my pressing season as hereinafter must they chirry will immedia-
tely pending on my safe return to ignorance and bliss with my ropes
of pearls for gamey girls the way you'll hardly know me. *(marginal: in our pretauratar Freda)* is post purification we will and render social service, missus.
Let us all aignite as amoseals and help our Jakeline sisters clean
up the hogshole. Burn only what's Irish, accepting their coals.
Write me *(L7)* very cursorily for Henrietta' sake on the life of jewvries
and the sludge of King Harrington's at its height running boulevards
over the whole of it. Bear in mind by Michael all the provincial's
bananas peels and eiacock eggs making drawadust jubilee along
Henry, Moore, Earl and Talbot streets. Luke at all the memmer
manning he'd dung for the pray of birds strewing the Castleknock
(verso White Fries) road and the Marist fathers eleven out on a rogation stag party.
Compaire them caponchin trowbers with the Bridge of Belches
in Fairview, east Dublin's favourite wateringplace and ump as you
jump it. Stand on, say, Aston's, I advise you strongly, along
quaith a copy of the Seeds and Weeds Act when you have procured
one for yourself and take a good longing gaze into any nearby
shopswindow you may select at suppose, let us say, the hoyth of
number eleven, Kane or Keogh's and in the course of about thirty-
two minutes'time proceed to turn aroundabout on your heehills
towards the previous causeway and I shall be very cruelly mista-
ken indeed if you will not be jushed astowshed to see how you will
be meanwhile durn weil topcested with cakes of slush occasioned by
the mush jam of the crosse and blackwalls traffic in transit. When
will the W. D. face of our muckloved city gets its wellbelavered
whitewish ? Who'll disasperaguss Pape's Avignue or who'll uproose
the Opian Way ? Tis an ill wee blows no poppy good. And fhis
labour's worthy of my higher. Do you know what, little girls ? One
of those days I am advised to positively strike off hiking for good
and all until such time as some mood is made to get me an increase
of automoboil and footwear as I sartunly think now, honest to
John, for an income of xos that that's about the sanguine boun-
dary limit. *(handwritten: x Sharon with Verse somewas)*

Sis dearest, Jaun added, melancholic this time whiles his onsa-
turncast eyes in stellar attraction followed swift to an imaginary
swellaw. O, the vanity of Vanissy ! All ends vanishing ! Personally.
Grog help me, I am in no violent hurry. If time enough lost the
ducks walking easy round them I'd turn back as sices as not if I
could only find the girl of my heart's appointment to guide me
by gastronomy under her safe conduct, I'd ask no kinder of fates
than to stay where I am, leaning on my cubits, at this passing
moment by localoption in the birds' lodging the pheasants among
ill well on into the bosom of the exhaling night, picking sto-
pandgo jewels out of the hedges and catching brilliants on the
tip of my wagger for them breezes zipping round by Drumsally

(handwritten bottom) I'll not tolk who'll brighton Bray and
a blue trus bait the Bell and never
worth our earth sport despair of Dublin dimtop that's more in my line.

(right margin handwritten annotations)
your essayest
but your priest mayor King merchant
Lns where's Cowtends Katecleam the woman with the muckrake
& musky, as he turned his dorse to he to make court to it, crawling with meniants & me. I'd right it all by moonself if I onl had been of my Holy Roy whom...

Maria's task was far from simple. One look at a proof corrected by Joyce makes that clear. When Sylvia Beach published Ulysses in 1922, the multiple corrections to the enormous work had practically ruined her. But in letting Joyce make them, she had undoubtedly helped him to achieve his masterpiece.

After working on the proofs,
the two friends chat for a while,
then set out for a walk.

Second

Day

Joyce

and

His

Publishers

Joyce arrives by taxi in front of Adrienne's bookshop.
They cross the street and go into Shakespeare and Co.

Adrienne opens the conversation by showing Joyce a picture of him taken just after his arrival in Paris in 1920.

May 1938: Joyce is sitting at the table on which he once spread the enormous manuscript of Ulysses. *Across from him sit Miss Beach and Mademoiselle Monnier, as he called them; Joyce was always very formal, even with his best friends. Sylvia Beach and Adrienne Monnier were his publishers in the twenties. Here they chat amicably; the bitterness of the past is forgotten—like that caused by Adrienne's letter to Joyce asking him no longer to consider Shakespeare and Co. as his office or Sylvia his secretary. Joyce was the first to realize that it had taken a great deal of courage for Miss Beach to publish* Ulysses, *which had been banned by the censors in English-speaking countries. The French translation published by Mademoiselle Monnier had opened the most exclusive literary circles of Paris to Joyce—they recognized him as a master of prose.*

*I was struck by the paleness of his features
and the fatigue in his voice.*

*Joyce, Adrienne, and Sylvia speak
with emotion of Valery Larbaud,
gravely ill at his home in Vichy. It
was Larbaud, a writer and a gifted
translator of English literature, who
had introduced Joyce to the French
public in a lecture given in 1921 at
La Maison des Amis des Livres—
the first time, according to Adrienne,
that a work written in English had
been analyzed in France by a French
writer before it had appeared in
England and the United States.*

Joyce seems to drift in a sea of silence.
Sylvia thinks of all those years in her life
that had been dedicated to the work of
the Irish writer.

They recall the time that Henri Matisse was approached about illustrating a deluxe American edition of Ulysses, *after the ban on publication had been lifted. The painter, not having read Joyce's work, referred to the poem by Homer and covered several pages with drawings inspired by Greek mythology. For the first time, I saw Joyce smile.*

Third

Day

Joyce

with

His

Family

Joyce had extremely fine hands.
He handled his ever-present cane
like a musical instrument.

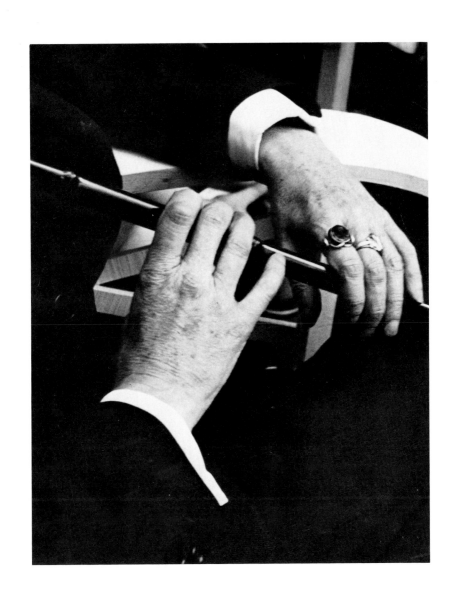

*Before going to visit his children,
he stops at a florist to buy
a carnation for his buttonhole.*

Joyce adored his children, Giorgio and Lucia—both born in Trieste—and his grandson, Stephen. His daughter had been living in a sanatorium for quite some time. Her mental illness deeply affected the author.

Giorgio lived with his wife, Helen, and their son in
a house on rue Scheffer, surrounded by a big
garden. Joyce did not insist that his wife appear in
the photographs, although he was very attached to
her. She herself remained loyal to Joyce from their
flight from Dublin in 1904 until his death in 1941.

To record for posterity four generations of his family,
Joyce had the idea of posing with Giorgio and Stephen
beneath the portrait of his father, John Stanislaus Joyce,
painted by the Irish artist Patrick Tuohy.

Later I photographed him playing the piano. Joyce loved to sing old Irish songs.

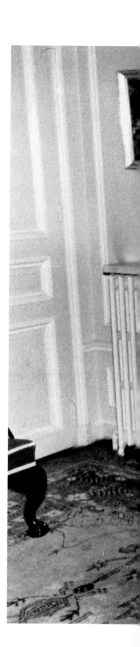

His son Giorgio had a beautiful bass voice, and Joyce hoped that he would become a professional singer.

*The assignment concluded, Gisèle Freund and
Eugene Jolas accompany Joyce to his home.*